*The
Course of
True Love . . .*

Grandma —

"War and Peace" it isn't.
But it _is_ between covers.
   Hope you like it.

         Love,
           Jon

The Course of True Love...

A Chronicle of Modern Romance

Jonathan Stone
Illustrations by Mary Adams

William Morrow and Company, Inc. | New York 1984

Text copyright © 1984 by Jonathan Stone
Illustrations copyright © 1984 by Mary Adams

All rights reserved. No part of this book may be
reproduced or utilized in any form or by any means, electronic
or mechanical, including photocopying, recording
or by any information storage and retrieval system, without
permission in writing from the Publisher. Inquiries
should be addressed to William Morrow and Company, Inc.,
105 Madison Avenue, New York, N.Y. 10016.

Library of Congress Cataloging in Publication Data

Stone, Jonathan.
The course of true love.

1. Love—Addresses, essays, lectures.   I. Title.
BF575.L8S84   1984   152.4   83-25080
ISBN 0-688-03185-4

Printed in the United States of America

First Edition

1 2 3 4 5 6 7 8 9 10

BOOK DESIGN BY LINEY LI

to **A.**,

to **C.**,

to **D.**,

to **J.**,

to **L.**,

to **S.** . . .

*The
Course of
True Love . . .*

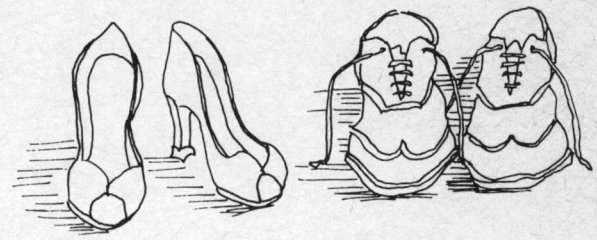

You've gone away on vacations together...

Party invitations now come addressed to the two of you...

When friends ask how you're doing, they always ask how she's doing too...

She talks comfortably on the phone to your parents...

Your friends tease you about being such a steady couple...

                                          And then...

Signs of Trouble . . .

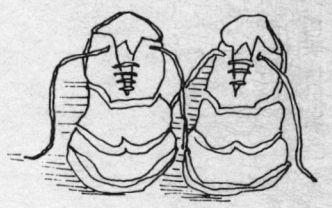

You're calling her more than she's calling you. Eventually, you notice it. You hadn't noticed it yet when the phone calls were running your two to her one. But when it got to three-to-one and four-to-one, you caught on to the cruel mathematics.

So you mention to her that she's allowed to call *you* once in a while. There is an odd silence after your remark, and the edges of the silence are tentatively examined by both of you.

You figure it's wise to even the balance. You resolve not to call her any more than she calls you. This requires tremendous will and resistance. Plenty of times, you half-dial her number. But you stay tough. And the phone calls stay perfectly balanced. The result is that now you two hardly talk at all.

There is other telephone evidence:

You call, and she asks if she can call you back in a couple of minutes. She's in the shower, in the middle of vacuuming, in the middle of something.

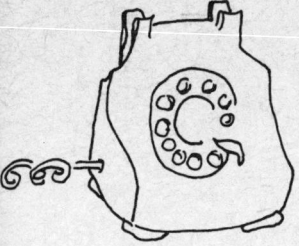

Your own telephone rings, you rush to it expectantly, and it is not her.

When you're at her place she doesn't exactly hurry off her telephone to be with you.

You put off getting together. It's late. You're both exhausted. You agree you'll get together tomorrow. This is how it's done in a stable relationship. But when you hang up, you hear the other tone in the conversation. A broader tiredness.

She sees old friends. Used to be, she'd try everything to put them off. She thought they were a nuisance, an intrusion on her life. Now she welcomes them. Visitors from her hometown, roommates from school, friends from her year in Europe, all stopping by, even staying over. They are an army—against what?

She has a drink with her old boyfriend. Just a drink. Just to see how he's doing. She hasn't *seen* him, hasn't even *spoken* to him in *so long*, and after all, she *did* go *out* with him for *two years*.

She returns in a few hours, completely trashed. They had nine drinks, she tells you merrily.

She falls asleep. This you once took to be a good sign. She would even fall asleep in your arms, her breath sweet against your face, and she was so beautiful sleeping, your happiness would flow, wet and silent, from your eyes.

The fact is, falling asleep with you there means you might as well *not* be there. So it's not such an unassailably good thing.

You watch her. She watches you. Suddenly there is assessment. The Greater Scheme of Things has entered the apartment, always a dangerous beast, though enter it must at some point.

These are not the short, overwhelmed, burst-out looks of lust and want with which you began. These are long stares, and a dullness etches into them.

The problem is, you're watching her only because she's watching you.

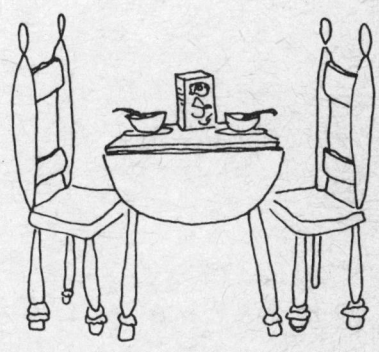

Other things take precedence for her. You've fallen into second. At best. Asked to make a conclusion about all this, you'd say you've been shifted down a notch. Maybe two. Probably this is merely the progress of a relationship. It settles in. Your passion and love cannot remain forever above other matters which deserve an equal share in a well-balanced life for her.

Like cleaning closets, doing the laundry, getting the groceries.

She'll call you later.

When Your Girlfriend Cries . . .

You are useless. You are incompetent. Your incompetence shows itself plainly, in case you believed you were finally overcoming it. You sit uselessly by, watching her cry. You don't know what to do. You can't just sit there and watch. Mechanically, you position your arm across her folded, heaving shoulders. Those beautiful shoulders. Is that all you can think of, those beautiful shoulders?

The moment your arm is securely in place, you realize—with a leaden certainty—that you've made a mistake. You withdraw your arm, rest for a moment, regroup.

You rub her back. You watch the gesture's feebleness. Your feeble hand drops away. Your hands are useless.

You don't know where to look. You look around the room. You can't just stare at her.

"Come on now," you say. A consolation stunning in its emptiness. As neutral as a light green sedan in the middle lane. "Come on now," you repeat in a soothing tone, knowing full well that soothing tone is all the phrase has going for it. "Come on now," you continue intermittently, uselessly, the words trotting off onto the vast horizon of your uselessness. "Come on now. Come on now . . ."

It is your fault. Rationally, it is not your fault at all. And she certainly doesn't believe it is your fault. But in life's deeper currents, where everything connects, you know you are directly responsible for her sobbing. If you were making her happy, she wouldn't be upset now. If you were making her happy, she wouldn't get upset about anything. You have failed her. This is abundantly clear in the single moment when she looks out from under her sobbing directly at you.

Her face contorts. Her features gather, like mourners at a funeral. Her eyes close up like bright nature at winter's onslaught. Her mouth turns down to spill sorrow resolutely. Her beautiful face distorts and twists and gnarls, and she looks, in an instant, like an old woman.

Her face is making its fist.

She looks ugly. And just the possibility of that ugliness, so swift and complete, gives you a swift moment of terror.

It proves your distance. In case you thought you had managed to get close, this certainly sets you straight. Watching her cry you realize you are nowhere near each other. You are fated to your opposite continents, divided by an infinite sea. You are destined, at best, to look across at her. You are destined not to know her, and probably she is destined not to know you. You watch her cry, and you have no idea who that is crying.

She proves her superiority. She's more sensitive than you. She is capable of more feeling. She is a higher form of the species. She is the maiden, crying alone by the brook, and you are the frog on the log, sitting dumbly by, simple-hearted, thoughtlessly watching.

When Your Girlfriend Leaves You . . .

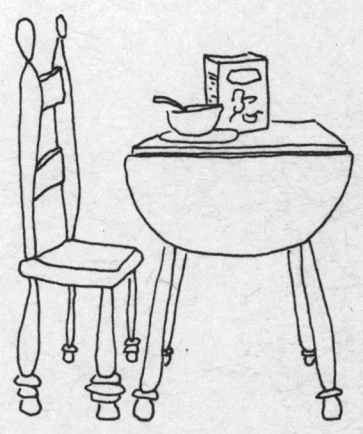

You become a genius. You get mild electrocutions of insight. You see deeper into life's moves, as if into moves of chess. Your mind hums in a new high gear. You understand what she meant when she said that, when she did that. There is the grid of her behavior. You wonder if geniuses and true artists live their whole lives in this mental agitation. You see connections in the world. You suffer exaggerated personhood. If there were only a way to focus all this insight on something useful, instead of ramming it continually against the dead-end stone wall of the facts.

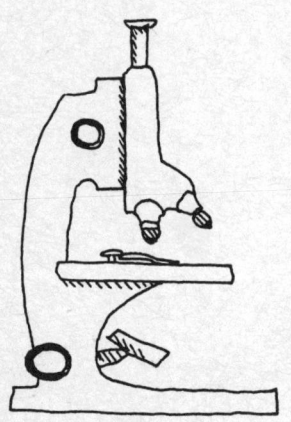

You tell a tale of woe. Over and over. Its details never fail to interest you. You see fresh nuances every time. You spill your soul to people you don't even like in real life. You shop for sympathy, pick it up like a shampoo on special. Soon enough, your tale takes on a philosophical tone. Inside, though, your guts are still in a triple Windsor.

Your friends don't know what to do. They listen to the tale. Over and over. They act interested in the details. They pull their own tales down off the shelf, polish them up and present them, just to show you're not alone. They know that doesn't help, they say. It just takes a little time, they say. Girls are like buses—you might miss one, but the next one comes along. Hey, it's poontang. It's twat. Listen, you don't own them, you know. Too many fish in the sea. None of these are true statements.

You believe in friendship again. A man needs friends. Sure, come on over tonight, he says. Beer and pizza. You get there. His girl is there, too. You don't mind Cindy here, do you?

You gotta have friends. You hang out. You tell your tale some more. Finally, he breaks. He finally agrees with you that you're a pathetic, miserable wretch.

Music might kill you. It is an exquisite torture. It seems possible you'll stop breathing during "Afternoon of a Faun." Top Forty suddenly shivers with meaning, the radio waves find an antenna along your spine. The lead singer seems to die a little more with every line. You put on the old stuff. Randy Newman is a seer. Shortly you make the rule for your roommate: No Music.

Your parents try to help. They know some girls. They seem to have stored girls at the backs of their memories, as if fully anticipating such a calamity. Each girl's name is pulled up by your parents' hopeful arched eyebrows. Each girl has a line of connection to you, rather than a physical appearance. Excitedly, your mother traces this line.

Your father asks you to go for a walk with him. He starts off rediscovering nature around the house. He doesn't mention the topic, but walks slowly enough and looks far enough down the road to prove his sympathy. It only proves to you his discomfort. Jesus, why couldn't the kid just hang onto his girlfriend, and spare me this?

Your parents try to help, and in their expertise as a subtle demoralizing force, make their first new advances in years.

Your wit evaporates. You're not funny. You're no longer the greatest guy in the world. You're a drag. You look out at the party from inside the psyche of a middle-aged Oklahoman. You feel your dullness—a slow, turning, insular peace—sort of nice, actually. You feel OK?, they ask. 'Cause you're a barrel of laughs.

The telephone poses a mortal threat. Its bell is an alarm that blacks out the city of your life processes—the avenues of your arteries, the interchange of your aorta, the glittering midtown of your thoughts. Its bell rings, and your heart attempts to answer it in a single leap out of your chest and throat.

You watch its next ring, to confirm the last one, and to prepare. Then your hand swoops to the receiver, a hawk's claw rending a limb from curled prey. It is someone else talking, and for the moments of your recovery, the miraculous mechanism fails: you honestly can't tell who it is or what they're saying.

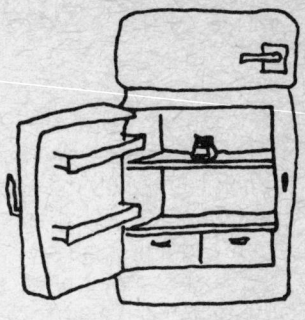

Everything else goes wrong, too. There is a sympathetic reaction across your world that accelerates logarithmically into a highly orchestrated conspiracy of nature, fate, and inanimate objects. Your work load is a drill press, flattening you into exhaustion. It's dark out when you finally leave the office. So you can't see that it's about to rain. From her balcony of heaven, Nature dumps her suds pail on your new herringbone suit. With a whimper of recognition, you burst toward the bus on the corner; with a revving of rage, it lurches from the corner without you. You reach the corner when a cab comes tight around it, and the fanning muddy splash drenches your herringbone pants and burrows into your shoes.

In the rain all the cabs are taken. All the stores around are closed. You can't stand there all night, freezing wet, waiting for the next bus. So you jog on. Another cornering cab scores across your thighs. You slog on.

In front of a restaurant you check your wallet. You forgot to go to the bank. You have three dollars. You're hungry. There's nothing at home to eat. But you could make it if that little store next door is open. It's not.

And the hunger gets hungry, begins to gnaw, and you trudge up to your apartment, you'll borrow money from your roommate, but he's not there, obviously, because the lights are off, and when you flip on the light switch, the bulb blows, and there are no extras, so you bring the one from your bedroom, and it blows, so it's the circuit, but the super's not home, and your neighbor's not there, and the apartment is dark, and the soaked suit is heavy like armor, and the hunger finds new places to feed, so you put on a raincoat, go back downstairs, go back out into the rain, and you trudge to the 7-Eleven, and you pick up a frozen dinner, and you trudge back, and come back upstairs, and you put the dinner in the oven, and you wait, and you wait, and you wait, but in the dark you turned the oven up too high, and you burn the frozen dinner to hard chips that even your desperation cannot bite through, and you toss the dinner into the garbage, but you miss the can, and in the dark—soaked, muddied, penniless, friendless, neighborless, hungry, exhausted—you bend down, to clean the burned dinner off the floor with toilet paper, since you're out of paper towels.

You feel around the pantry, and you find some crackers, and you take off your wet herringbone, and lie naked in the bed, in the dark, eating crackers, till someone comes to rescue you.

Somewhere, somehow, trash cans and light bulbs, frozen dinners and muddy puddles, buses, and the thundering heavens themselves must be in collusive celebration.

Things are bad.

*Your Loneliness
Is Confirmed* . . .

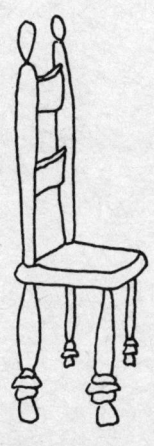

Observing happy couples. You see them everywhere. Transforming a crowded subway car into an ironic set for their affection. Appropriating a block of sidewalk for the physical proclamations of their good fortune. You walk past row upon row of them, sitting at small white-linened tables along restaurant windows, leaning toward one another, punctuating stories, leaning back, smiling. Row upon row upon row of them, slumped into their closeness at movie theaters. You see them all. You don't miss a couple, don't miss a glance. You share every tender moment of theirs. You're Cupid disguised in a trench coat. You know things about them. You know, for instance, that she is way too good-looking for him. You follow couples down the street. Follow them to where they enter restaurants together, where they enter apartments together. Follow them to a corner where, lightly brushing one another—wordless, tender assurance—they part.

Then you follow her.

Step right into line behind those taut calves. You are a spy. A perfect occupation, because you feel you do not, in any serious way, exist.

Seeing your best friend's new baby girl. He leans over the crib, and turns his head to face hers. He takes up the familiar glowing specimen in a confident stroke. She is wide-eyed at her swift ride heavenward. As she is wrapped into his arms, so he wraps himself into her being.

You, the welcome visitor and proud wanderer of moments ago, are suddenly absented. Trishia stands in the shadow, against the door jamb, arms crossed, a slight smile, proudly satisfied with that love again witnessed. The shadow of the doorway warms, for love is once more from that vantage assured.

The tiny baby is the visible clasp—smooth and rounded—that ties the invisible ribbons of theory and love.

The three of them are one package now. There is simply them and everything else. This is most clear when you are standing close, as if asked to hold a gift that is not yours, uncomfortably waiting for someone to take it from you.

You look at them. This is what it's all about. The rest is nonsense. You, of course, are still a high-rent tenant of said nonsense.

In the light of Sunday afternoon. There is a certain slant of light, in the few hours before the evening closes over. A cold light, a fact, upon the sandstone buildings and monuments. A light that holds the late afternoon still, and then grows timid. The slanted light rouses the half-world of thoughts. They cross groggy. What a nice light for a walk with her. A walk in late Sunday afternoon. Just a walk with her. Just a walk, talking away like you used to do, walking silently like you used to do, just a long long walk through the slanted light, past the monuments, past the trees, past everything, instead of watching a golf tournament on NBC.

When *your neighbor goes into her apartment and you go into yours.* You talk pleasantly on the elevator, neighbors. You're funny. She laughs. Says more. The elevator arrives. Still talking, she goes to her door, fumbles with her keys. Still talking, you go to your door, fumble with your keys. You both look over your shoulders, still talking. She concocts an appropriate line—some half-baked, half-intelligent semifinality that gives you both the moment to exit.

You're not one for sexual anarchy, but she is so pretty, and now she's going to pour herself a drink, cook something up for herself, watch TV, talk on the phone. But she's *got* to be thinking the same as you. Why doesn't anybody say anything? Why doesn't she invite you in? Why don't you invite her in? You close your apartment door.

You lie on your bed, and flip through radio stations. You walk up and down. You rattle around your apartment for hours. She rattles around hers for hours. For you hear her television. You hear her on the phone. Her rattling around pretends to more organization than yours. Yours makes no pretensions.

Soon enough she must hear your television. She must hear you on the phone.

Patterns are mightier than armored divisions.

When you're set up on a blind date, and you fantasize not only her incredible good looks but a life together.

I mean, come on.

YOUR LONELINESS IS CONFIRMED . . . 40

Running into your old girlfriend on the street. (Part A: You see her first.) This is a disaster. This is the second-to-worst disaster that life has to offer.

You see her. Your heart pounds a single drumbeat that sends the message across the sleepy terrains of mind and body. You prepare your new personality, the one she wanted you to have. You will stand guard over the traits she couldn't handle. You told her you could change—you quickly align those great changes now, prepare to make them obvious.

She sees you. She smiles. You forget to smile at first. Then you remember to. She comes closer. How are you. How are you. Looking her over intently, searching her hair, her hands, her mind-numbing features, you forget about the new personality. And then your time is up. She has to run. She gives you a solider look in the eyes. To show you she cares. She goes. You watch her continue down the street. She does not turn to see you. But she knows you're watching. Once again, she has left you alone.

Running into your old girlfriend on the street. (Part B: She sees you first.) THIS is the worst disaster life has to offer. She surprises you from the side. "Hi!" You turn. Terror crosses you, your terror mirrors in her face. You try to recover, to wipe the mirror clean. But the situation is unrecoverable. The good fortune of a chance meeting, the chance you've dreamed of, irretrievable right off the bat. She looks frightened by her mistake. She feels awful. She feels guilty. Animatedly, you talk to the guilty. Full of fun and funny stories, you try to entertain a criminal who has just confessed to manslaughter. Not the most receptive audience.

She walks away. You watch her continue down the street. She feels, of course, that she cannot turn to see you. You watch her, a mythical creature, returning to the human ocean, its waves closing around her now on the busy sidewalk. Once again, she has left you alone.

So There You Are . . .

In a discotheque. You don't use the term "discotheque." The term discotheque, after all, would imply 1965 French girls in minidresses, sweating and dancing, crowded under flashing lights, constantly smiling for invisible *paparazzi.*

Here there *are* some French girls in minidresses, sweating and dancing, crowded under the flashing lights, constantly smiling for invisible *paparazzi.*

You watch the mechanical processes—the braces and hinges—above the flashing lights. Somehow the lighting effects don't seem to work so well. The music seems undone, too. You hear the hissing and buzzing of the speakers beneath and between the songs. Something's not wired right.

You adopt cool. You stand with a foot up on the

rail. You certainly appear lost in fascinating thought. You drink your drink slowly, experienced. Each sip is measured, and fully, independently deserved.

The electric guitar rages through the interior. The bass pounds against your chest. The drumbeat is like a giant's footsteps.

Finally, you lean forward to a girl's ear to deliver your funny line over the music. It seems you shout it at yourself.

She couldn't hear a word.

You look expressionlessly at each other.

She walks away.

But it's a start. It's easier now. You move from area to area of the disco, from ripe field to ripe field. You are one of the hungry.

At a big party. The door opens onto a horror-movie transmutation. The darkened apartment is overrun by a seething larval mass. It surges in the living room, infests the kitchen, infects the bedrooms. A Beach Boys sound track increases the horror, though the sound is tinny and weak, swallowed up meanly by the seething mass. As always, for a moment your impulse is to shut the door and stay outside in the hall. As always, you shoulder in to the center of the beast.

There is a long conversation with someone you unfortunately know well: his job, his girlfriend, movies, apartment rents again. While he talks, you watch the girl across the room, long enough to see someone else move in to talk to her. As always, you've slipped thoughtlessly into your oldest patterns, firmed up ineradicably and forever.

The can of beer seems to sweat its alcohol into your hand, for soon it's not beer but warm liquid you're drinking. You manage to get away from the conversation, move once through the party, and then your friend corners you again.

Soon come the joints, orange embers floating shoulder level, like beacons to a paradise that lurks close and tempting. No joints circle to you.

You run into another old friend.

At a small dinner party. The hostess opens the door, and even before your pleasantries, with razor vision you execute a survey of the women throughout the room behind her, and based on the results of that lightning assessment, the party is over for you.

Drawing the celery stalk and loading it with guacamole dip, you confirm it with a count of the women, the men, and the chairs at the table. Sure enough. Everyone is here. The party's over.

You bite into the celery. Hope is destroyed loudly in your mouth.

Of course, you are the hit of the party. You're a charmer. Half the girls later asked the hostess for your number, she tells you. Terrific.

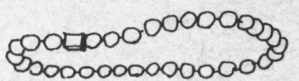

In the living room of a girl's apartment at three in the morning. The casual tilt of the drink in your hand, your casual posture, could not be more deceitful. For while you were exhausted an hour ago, now you're fully alert, attentive, tuned to every second. To anyone else, the living room would appear quietly lit. To you, it is brightly flooded with light. A psychological fluorescence lights the precise surgery looming.

Once again, two opposite worlds balance on the fulcrum of a kiss. Tonight you have edged slowly up the beam with tangoing conversation, with wit and charm a-tap-tapping, and you wait poised and awkwardly balanced on the fulcrum, with the beam now horizontal, ready to fall easily into the darker, private realm of emotion, passion, need— the unspoken. The beam, wavering now, precarious, waiting for the single kiss to send it over.

A funneling down to the point of the kiss, and beyond it, a widening out again, into great reaches where stars float . . .

And she must be watching the fulcrum as closely as you . . .

Only a kiss, just a kiss . . .

In the bathroom of a girl's apartment at nine in the morning. Strange-looking fixtures. The sink's hot and cold faucets will not hold the temperatures you set. The shower coughs and drools and tries and gives out, inferior. The strange brand of shampoo, its better scent, its nicer feel in your palm. The pink plastic razor, light blond leg hairs still in it. You pull the hairs and set them into the toilet carefully, like the reefweeds of the raft you're building Moses. Lathering palmfuls of soap, setting them evenly on your beard, for want of shaving cream. The lightness of the hollow razor across your face, its seashell echo with each scrape. Watching, absently attentive, tentative, as the toilet barely flushes but comes up clean. The rituals of your life, changed and charged now.

You look in the mirror. Sure enough—incredibly—it is you there in that girl's bathroom. You feel like you're someone else. Someone . . . smoother.

You feel odd.

Possible Topics of Discussion on a First Date

Your ambitions, your dreams. Let's face it, the career choices of best-selling novelist, revolutionary, and artist in an island paradise have lost credibility finitely and measurably, with every passing hour of every passing year, since they first seemed gloriously true possibilities on dates when you were seventeen. But incredibly enough, the belief, the *conviction* with which you present your dreams seem to be what interests a woman, although she certainly suspects some of the dreams are growing ever more unlikely of coming to pass. You see, it was never the specific dream, as you once thought, it was, rather, the spirit of the dream. Thus liberated, you can make yourself anything. Don't worry about backing it up with facts and credibility. Just show it's deep in you, and there could be more deep in you where that came from.

Your family. This is a tricky one. There are two ways to go here. One says it's best to be a desperado who rides in off the desert, out of nowhere, unlit match in teeth, kin to a miracle or a force of nature. On the other hand, life may be risky enough for a girl without these pastless types. A man from a family is trustworthy, responsible—might even have some dough. A bastion against the world.

In this case, just a mention should do it. No family stories. Listen to anyone else tell one, and let it be a lesson to you. And keep her from telling any. It'll keep her from being embarrassed by her boring you, and she'll enjoy her own sprung-whole-from-the-desert desperado status. It makes her feel freer.

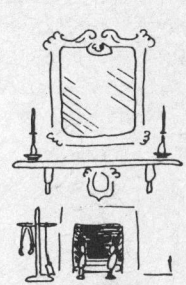

Any topic that leads you gracefully into a discussion of sex. Good restaurants, favorite old TV shows, absurd apartment prices, your exercise regimen: the standard topics loom up like prison walls. You contemplate a life sentence of polite conversation.

Seize the moment. Try, instead, topics of the Mind. Man's sixth sense, instincts, cases of your own ESP, of her ESP, her dreams last night, your dreams last night, ghosts, the occult, fire away! Since the Mind remains a frontier, you can both speculate without being undone by the other, because everything said is valid, because nobody knows anything. And most important of all, the topic of the Mind is a great segue into fantasy, and from there, a short skip into the always engaging topic of sex.

What men really want, what women really want. Also a good one, since everything either of you says is valid—coming from an authority, after all. This can reveal her to you. Unfortunately, it's not your area of expertise, as you've proved again and again. Proceed carefully, and pick up her cues.

Your past relationships. The fascinating tale of your life and loves is a lot less fascinating to her—and everyone else—than it is to you. When you say reverently, sweetly, "She was a dancer," the statement does not hold the same sense of revelation for your date that it does for you. Do not indicate how your life organizes itself completely around your relationships. Do not say "she was." Say "she is," if the issue comes up. Show your broad view, that relationships are a matter of process, gentle waves on currents of a continuous sparkling stream. Try not to laugh. Try not to cry.

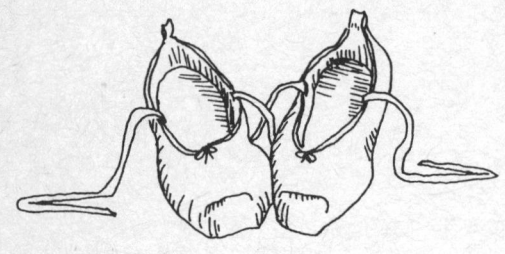

*When
You're Falling
in Love . . .*

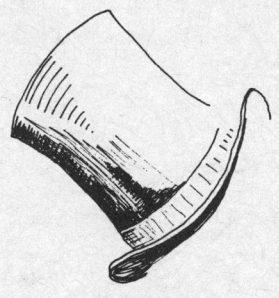

*Y*ou smile suddenly as you walk down the street. It is a reflex. Beyond your conscious control. The sides of your mouth ride up. You notice it, you notice others noticing it, but you can't control the smile.

You are overcharged with energy, filled with uncontainable good feeling. You struggle to contain your good feeling in a civilized walk.

You start laughing out loud. It is again a reflex. You hear yourself laugh, but it is beyond your conscious control. Now you are a public spectacle.

Some of the people think you're smiling at them. They smile back.

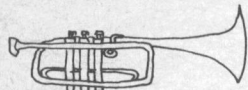

All right! It's like you've won a baseball game. The flush of victory. That face of hers. God!!! You're smiling again.

Everything goes well. You get things done. You have this new smooth mastery over your work. The daily demands of your life—organizing, decision making—become effortless.

You make plans. There are places you want to see with her, things you want to do with her. You're no longer so contented lying alone on your bed.

You loosen up. You start bantering and joking with the girls at the office, playing those verbal-games-in-passing that are so detestable when overheard and so witty as a participant. You start talking to girls walking on the street. You ask girls questions at the supermarket. You ask girls questions at the bus stop. You have no dark motives for all this, particularly, but everyone is so *approachable*. Human contact seems so natural.

Out in the world, you're comfortable. The outside world seems to belong to you especially. You're overcome by your own sense of omnipotence. It scares you.

The day seems arranged for your amusement. You're a major stockholder on a tour of the plant.

*Y*ou *are normal.* You've joined the flow. You're a full participant. You're on track. You feel certainty. You've got a girl.

You are joined to a biological and psychological order endorsed by pop psychologists. You are the strived-for result of self-help books.

You've got a girl. It gives you something to do. It gives you somewhere to go.

You've got a girl.

You reach for her. With no forethought, no calculation to your affections, you reach for her. It is not to give or receive pleasure on some scale. It is done without that moment of consideration. You notice it only after you already are touching her, if you notice it consciously at all. It's no longer just sex. It's digging in deeper.

Life seems good. At first, you regard this as a temporary delusion. The next day will surely correct it. But the good days string together. The bad days are soon way past due. The evidence is overwhelming: these are good times.

Empirically speaking, there will be bleak times again. But these will again be followed by good times. Which will again be followed by bleak times. Good, bad, good, bad. You've seen how that's the story.

Then again, the right person would change that pattern. Easily. Forever.

And you're feeling awfully good right now.

Is this the one?

Maybe.

Maybe not.

But maybe.